The Little Book Of Positivity

Kelly Robinson-Key

ISBN: 978-1-9162583-0-3

kellyrobinsonkey@gmail.com

www.kellyrobinsonkey.com

Thank You

I thank my husband for encouraging me to write and supporting me on this wonderful journey.

I thank my children for being my inspiration, and having so much patience whilst I work.

I thank everyone around me for encouraging me to publish my poems and have confidence in myself.

And I thank you, the reader, for taking your time to read my book. I hope that it brings you positive thoughts when you need them the most.

Contents

Start The Day

The best way

to start the day,

is thinking in

a positive way.

I Need

I need coffee, I need tea,

I need time just for me.

I need chocolate, I need cake,

I need a spa break.

I need cocktails, I need wine,

I need time in the sunshine.

Mental Health

We need to look after

our mental health.

It is more important

than any amount of wealth.

Meditation, exercise,

communication, and sleep.

Write something positive

each day of the week.

Do these things and

I think you'll find,

these are the things

that will help your mind.

Not Alone

You are not alone,

I am here too.

I will never give up,

On someone like you.

Eyes

You are worth
more than
you believe.
Just open your
eyes and see.

Be You

Be you,

Be strong,

Be kind,

Be free.

Be the person

you want to be

Forward To Happiness

Looking back brings
heartache and pain.
Remembering things
again and again.
Forget the past and
turn yourself around.
Look forward and happiness
will be found.

Be Kind

A smile and a hug can move
clouds from another's mind.
Take time to talk to others
and always be kind.

Believe

Believe and you will see

the happiness that's

meant to be.

Hopes And Dreams

Clouds are full of hopes

and dreams.

When it rains love fills

the streams.

No Regrets

The sun rises and the sun sets.

Make it a day with no regrets.

Start with a smile and

a positive thought.

Carry the shine that

The sun has brought.

More Than

Braver, stronger, wiser, and bolder.

Things I feel now I'm older.

Love, happiness, peace, and health.

Things that now mean more than wealth.

You've Got This

You can do this, more than you know.

You have watched people come and go.

You don't need them to help you stand.

You are strong, you don't need a hand.

Don't break down and think they have won.

Stand tall and show them you are the sun.

Keep looking forward, you will be fine.

You have come this far, now is your time.

Rain

No colour would be seen in a world without rain.

A world without tears would be

a world without pain.

A world without pain would be

a world without love.

The world needs the rain,

that comes from up above.

Stop Saying When

Your life is a story.

You have control over the pen.

You just need to start writing,

and stop saying when.

Life Is Hard

Life is hard.

Be kind to yourself.

Look after your mind,

the same as you

look after your health.

Kindness

Kindness is always needed,

each and every day.

It removes negativity

and takes the pain away.

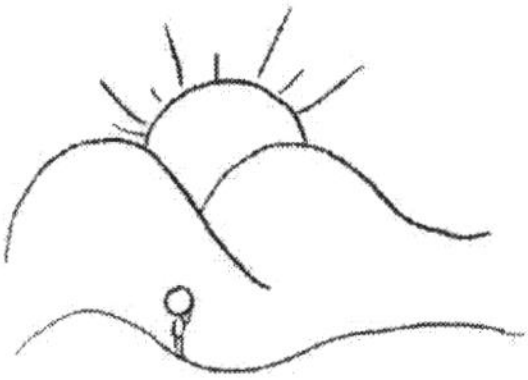

Fresh View

New year, new beginnings, new start, fresh view.

A time for change, a time to focus,

Now is the time for a new you.

Life And Love

Life and love go through waves,

Waves that follow the moon.

When it's at its fullest,

Your passion will surely bloom.

A Strong Woman

A strong woman has a strong mind.

A mind of her own that is courageous and kind.

Don't take her for granted.

Don't break her heart.

Her inside beauty is a work of art.

Skipping Feet

Wandering free so I can be
wild like the waves out at sea.
A stick in my hand, wind in my hair.
My skipping feet will take me there.

Don't Be Afraid Of The Dark

Don't be afraid of the dark,

when the moon is there to show

that there is beauty in the dark,

with its bright and beautiful glow.

Be Like The Sun

Why be so serious
when there is fun?
Smile and laugh,
and be bright
like the sun.

Stars And Moon

Stars sparkle in the night,
next to the moon
shining bright.
They guide us to where
we are meant to be.
To tomorrow's sun
that will set us free.

Happy

You can't please everyone,
but try and please just you.
If you make yourself happy,
then others will be happy too.

Take Time

Taking time out of my day,

to rest my body and dream away.

Imagining places warmed by the sun.

Dancing, singing, having fun.

We must remember to take some time,

to rest our body, soul and mind.

Give Yourself Time

Sometimes we need just a few days,

to step back from our normal ways.

To think about life and where we are going.

Give yourself time to get ideas flowing.

Sometimes things don't go to plan,

but this is ok, find a way that can.

Work hard, but give yourself time.

Time to yourself, you will be fine.

Sacrifice

Losing direction, focus fades.

Emotions come strong, like the sea waves.

Don't sacrifice your happiness for others joy.

Life is too short to let them destroy.

Plant The Seed

Give what you can.
Take what you need.
Eat the tree's apple.
Then plant the seed.

Don't Look Back

Find the right tune.

Dance to the right track.

Headphones in.

Don't look back.

Writing Can Change The World

Writing can change the world to love from hate.
Think before you speak,
be kind when you communicate.
Words can cut deeper than you know.
A sharp tongue can be as deadly
as a bow and arrow.
Be kind, love hard, never stop believing.
There can be peace in the world that we live in.

My Place

I've spent my life trying to find my place,

on this blue planet, surrounded by space.

As I get older I begin to realise,

my place is right here

in front of my eyes.

Great Outdoors

Breathing in air from the great outdoors.

Taking in oxygen where the eagle soars.

Helps to relax your soul and mind.

Leaving all the negatives from the world behind.

Take A Breath

Being tested to your limit makes you strong
when you need to be.
Take a deep breath, think a happy thought
and things will work out fine you'll see.

Headphones In

Laying on my bed in the deep of the night.

Headphones in, stars shining bright.

Chilling to the sounds from music I adore.

Thinking of my future and what life has instore.

Dreaming big and of places I want to go.

Humming the tune of the song on low.

This is my favourite time of the day.

Relaxing my mind, where I lay.

Freedom

Freedom is felt when you dance in the rain.

Feeling the drops removes the pain.

Put your hands out to the side.

Be brave, don't hide.

Today is the start of something new.

Forget the past, find a happy you.

Sky

Tell the sky your dreams and she will

keep them safe for you.

She will return them when it's time,

for your dreams to come true.

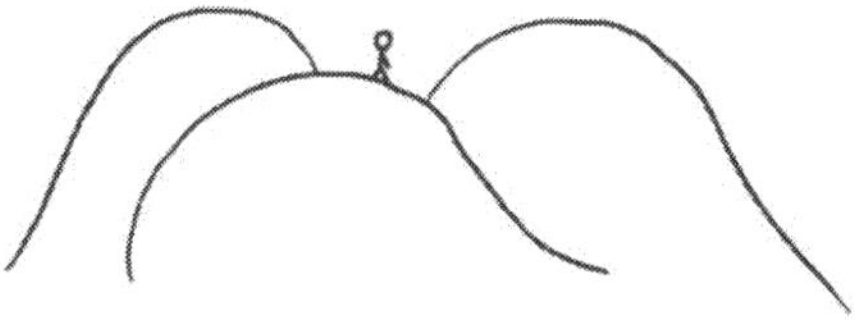

Head To The Hills

The world is full of beautiful places.

Kind people with smiling faces.

Don't focus on the negative or on the bad.

This will only make you angry and sad.

When you get down, head for the hills.

Take in the fresh air from the valleys and fields.

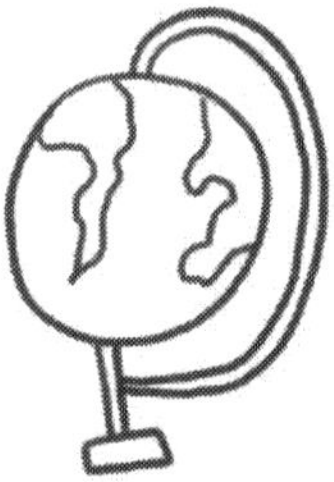

In The Fast Lane

Live life on the edge.

Travel in the fast lane.

Go see the world,

then see it again.

Don't be put off.

Don't follow society.

Do what you want to do.

Go wild, be free.

Win

Life is not about making others happy,

but finding happiness from within.

Love yourself,

be kind to your mind,

and at life you will

always win.

Be You

Try something new.

Always be true.

Believe in yourself.

Be you.

Speaking

Speaking about your worries and fears,
is a very scary thing.
Admitting you aren't coping well
and you're struggling.
But opening up to others,
speaking about what is wrong,
will make you feel a whole lot better.
The darkness won't last for long.

Walk Out

Walk out of the room.

Leave it all behind.

Clear your head

Empty your mind.

Sometimes we just need

space and time.

A few more minutes

and all will be fine.

Happy

Chocolate and cake.

Coffee and tea.

A good book.

Time for me.

Candles and a bath.

A film on TV.

These are the things,

that make me happy.

Be Humble

A pen and a pencil will write the same words.

Beautiful songs can be heard from the birds.

A bus or a car will get you to the same place.

Life is a fun journey not a competitive race.

So be humble and appreciate what you have today.

Love the life you live and do it your own way.

Spring Days

Sunflowers and bumblebees,
fresh air, green leaves.
Sitting on the grass
feeling the sun rays,
on these warm spring days.

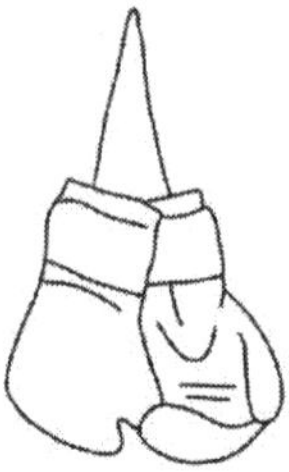

Fighting

Keep on fighting.

Never give in.

They will bully you,

don't let them win.

Your voice will be heard.

Your strength will shine through.

You can do this.

Don't let them break you.

Autumn

Candles lit, fire on.

Summers days are almost gone.

Autumn leaves falling down.

The green trees turning brown.

These are the days I like the most.

Cosy blankets, Sunday roast.

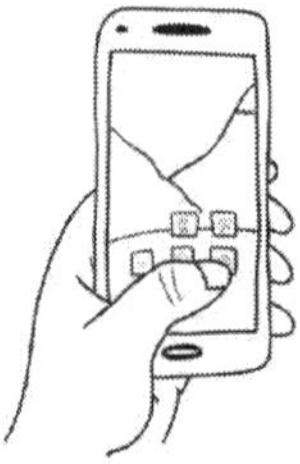

Our Minds

Our minds were designed to be outside,

in the woods or by the tide.

They weren't designed to work long hours,

in office blocks, in tall towers.

They weren't designed for busy schedules,

working lunches, strict rules.

They weren't designed to be staring at apps,

glued to a screen whilst the thumb taps.

Our mind wasn't designed for a world like this.

it needs to be outside

where nature is.

Aim For The Stars

Others don't understand the dream that you see.
They will knock you down like gravity.
Go against the grain, just ignore.
Remove yourself from the floor.
Stay focused and keep on going.
Aim for the stars that keep on glowing.

Take That Step

Focusing on what you desire,

helps you fight like fire on fire.

Taking that step when you're most afraid,

pennies are lost but fortunes are made.

Follow that dream, never give in.

The harder you work,

the more you'll win.

You Can Do It

You can do it

if you put your

mind to it.

Time To Reflect

Time to reflect

and time to plan.

Time to take your career,

as far as you can.

What will this year bring?

Nobody knows.

Let's see how far

this passion river flows.

Your Way

Do you have a focus?

A place you aim to go?

How will you get there?

Do you even know?

If you're at a crossroads

and don't know which way to turn.

Research the stories of others,

it's the best way to learn.

A route you must plan,

before you start your journey.

You will get there in time,

just focus your energy.

Dream Big

Dream big in a world

full of opportunities.

Don't be afraid of

your insecurities.

Unique

You are unique.

Each star is too.

Don't be afraid

to shine like they do.

Sunrises

Sunrises and sunsets.

Live a day with no regrets.

Start with a plan.

Follow your heart.

Be motivated right

from the start.

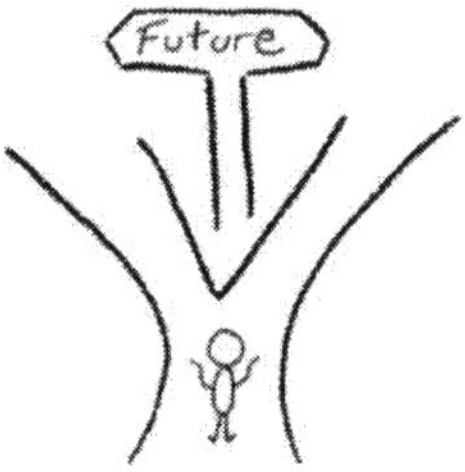

The Right Path

Make mistakes.

Take the wrong turn.

Step close to the fire,

but don't let it burn.

It takes time and courage too,

to find the right path in life for you.

Wandering Mind

Unable to stay focused, a wandering mind.

All these ideas I seem to find.

I want to try and do them all.

But is it really possible?

There is only one way to know for sure.

To try each idea and then try some more.

Little People

Little people with big voices,

scare those that

make the choices.

Follow Your Heart

It is ok to be different.

It is ok to stand out.

Others won't like it.

They may scream and shout.

Just ignore them.

Do what's right for you.

Follow your heart

and your dreams will come true.

Creativity

Don't drown in the negativity.

Use it to grow your creativity.

Butterfly

A butterfly will land on the flower,
even though it could be eaten.
So don't be afraid to reach your goal,
even though you could be beaten.

Fire Within

The fire burns within, so let it begin.

Your adventure to freedom.

Dreams you need to free them.

The stars call your name.

The sun's doing the same.

Start it today.

What do you say?

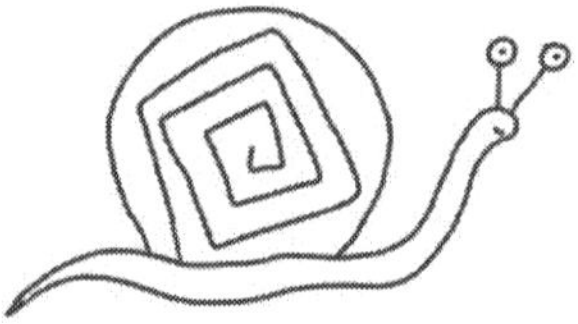

Our Own Pace

Sometimes we need to move slow,
move at our own pace.
We will reach our own goal,
it's a personal race.
Don't look to others,
to see how far they've come.
Focus on your path,
enjoy it, have fun.

Take The Gamble

Don't be scared of new beginnings.

Take the gamble and reap the winnings.

Future Is In Your Hands

Time spent sitting and hoping
that your dreams will come true
is wasted time when there
are other things you could do.
Take the first step.
Start making plans.
From this day forward
your future is in your hands.

Fear

An exciting life waits for you at the end of fear.

You just need to be brave enough,

this is your year.

Career

Finding a focus, knowing what to do.

Trying to find a career that is perfect for you.

Is not that easy when there is so much choice.

You just need to sit down and listen to your voice.

What do you want in this life that is short?

Should you continue doing

what you have been taught?

Or try a new path and find a new career.

Don't be afraid, ignore the fear.

Grab a pen and paper,

list the things you love.

You will soon find a way

to your stars up above.

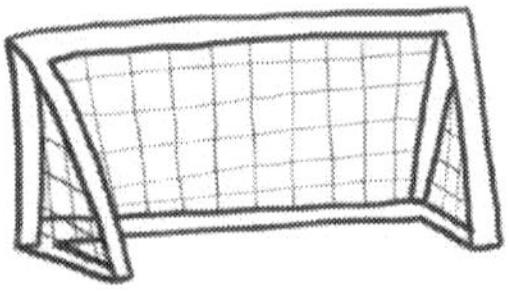

Your Goal

It takes courage and strength to turn your back,
but others opinion's can lead to the wrong track.
Don't follow their ideas if
they don't match your own.
You can follow your dream even if you're alone.
Focus on your goal,
ignore what others say.
It won't be long before you
make it your own way.

Kelly Robinson-Key is a writer and illustrator that creates educational and inspirational rhymes. After suffering from post-natal depression, Kelly found that writing positive rhymes helped her to recover and think more positively about the world around her. She lives in the picturesque Welsh valleys with her husband, two children, and their pug called Lloyd.

For more information please visit
www.kellyrobinsonkey.com